This Is Me

Facing Physical Challenges

ABDO
Publishing Company

This Is Me

Facing Physical Challenges

by Stephanie Watson

Content Consultant
Dr. Robyn J. A. Silverman
Child/Teen Development Expert and Success Coach
Powerful Words Character Development

Credits

Published by ABDO Publishing Company, 8000 West 78th Street, Edina, Minnesota 55439. Copyright © 2010 by Abdo Consulting Group, Inc. International copyrights reserved in all countries. No part of this book may be reproduced in any form without written permission from the publisher. The Essential Library™ is a trademark and logo of ABDO Publishing Company.

Printed in the United States.

Editor: Melissa Johnson
Copy Editor: Amy Van Zee
Interior Design and Production: Nicole Brecke
Cover Design: Becky Daum

Library of Congress Cataloging-in-Publication Data
Watson, Stephanie, 1969-
  This is me : facing physical challenges / by Stephanie Watson ; content consultant, Robyn J. A. Silverman.
      p. cm. — (Essential health : strong, beautiful girls)
  Includes index.
  ISBN 978-1-60453-753-6
  1. Disabilities. 2. Body image. 3. Self-control. I. Title.
  HV1568.T46 2010
  613'.04243—dc22
                                        2009002136

Contents

Meet Dr. Robyn

Dr. Robyn Silverman loves to spend time with young people. It's what she does best! As a child and adolescent development specialist, Dr. Robyn has devoted her time to helping girls just like you become all they can be. Throughout the Strong, Beautiful Girls series, you'll hear her expert advice as she offers wisdom on boyfriends, school, and everything in between.

An award-winning body image expert and the creator of the Powerful Words Character System, Dr. Robyn likes to look on the bright side of life. She knows how tough it is to be a young woman in today's world, and she's prepared with encouragement to help you embrace your beauty even when your "frenemies" tell you otherwise. Dr. Robyn struggled with her own body image while growing up, so she knows what you're going through.

Dr. Robyn has been told she has a rare talent—to help girls share their wildest dreams and biggest problems. Her compassion makes her a trusted friend to many girls, and she considers it a gift to be able to interact with the young people who she sees as the leaders of tomorrow. She even started a girls' group, the Sassy Sisterhood Girls Circle, to help young women pinpoint how media messages impact their lives and body confidence so they can get healthy and get happy.

As a speaker and a success coach, her powerful messages have reached thousands of people. Her expert advice has been featured in Prevention magazine, Parents magazine, and the Washington Post. She was even a guest editor for the Dove Self-Esteem Fund: Campaign for Real Beauty. But she has an online presence too, and her writing can be found through her blogs, www.DrRobynsBlog.com and www.BodyImageBlog.com, or through her Web site, www.DrRobynSilverman.com. Dr. Robyn also enjoys spending time with her family in Massachusetts.

Dr. Robyn believes that young people are assets to be developed, not problems to be fixed. She's out to help you become the best you can be. As she puts it, "I'm stepping up to the plate to highlight news stories gone wrong, girls gone right, and programs that help to support strengths instead of weaknesses. I'd be grateful if you'd join me."

Take It from Me

When I was in school, I had a good friend named Carl who was deaf. I never thought twice about the fact that Carl couldn't hear, because he was one of the coolest kids I knew. He could read lips, so I could have verbal conversations with him as long as I looked at him when I spoke.

Although I never saw Carl as being different, I also never stopped to think about what it was like for him to be deaf. Did it ever bother him not to be able to hear? Was it harder for him to go to school? Did he ever feel left out?

At almost every school, there is at least one person like Carl who is dealing with a physical issue. They may be overweight, nearsighted, have a condition such as asthma or diabetes, or use a wheelchair. No matter what his or her situation is, you can be sure that person has felt different from the other kids at some point.

Although I was good friends with Carl, I know there were many other classmates with physical issues who I totally overlooked. I remember one girl who was in special education. Her locker was near mine, yet I don't think I ever talked to her or even made eye contact. There was also a guy who needed special braces to walk. I never once stopped to say hello or find out what he was like.

Looking back, I regret that I didn't take the time to get to know those classmates. If I had talked to them, I probably would have found out that we had a lot in common. We might have become friends. In fact, we might still be friends today.

In this book, you'll meet nine girls who are living with physical issues. If you're dealing with one of these issues, I hope this book will give you more confidence in yourself and your abilities. If you know people who are dealing with these issues, maybe you'll start to look at them in a different way. And maybe someday when you look back at this time in your life, you won't feel like you missed out on a possible friend.

XOXO,
Stephanie

1

The Big Girl

Many women and girls today struggle with their weight. Busy families eat out more frequently than they did in the past. Restaurant portion sizes are growing larger, and people are consuming more sugary snacks and sodas. At the same time, many girls are less active than children were in the past. The more time you spend sitting in front of the television or computer, the less time you have to get outside and work out or play sports.

Everyone wants to fit in, and that can be hard to do when you're a different size than all of your friends. Kids at school can be really cruel. They may tease people who are overweight, calling them names or accusing them of being lazy or sloppy—neither of which is true.

Being overweight can be hard on your self-esteem, but it's even harder on your body. According to medical doctors, overweight kids are more likely to get diseases such as asthma, heart disease, and a type of diabetes. They're also more likely to be overweight when they grow up, making them even more prone to these diseases. Destiny had been overweight most of her life, but she had no idea how much of a risk that extra weight was posing to her health.

Destiny's Story

Destiny was used to being called names. "Hey fatty!," "Yo, big butt!," and "Tubby!" were just a few of the things the jocks at school would shout at her as she walked through the halls. She acted like she was beyond caring, but it really did hurt.

Destiny had never been thin. She'd never been able to fit into slim jeans like her best friend, Kim. Usually, Destiny **Being overweight can be hard on your self-esteem, but it's even harder on your body.** wore baggy shirts to try hiding her stomach and hips. Every woman in her family struggled with her weight. Destiny's mother went on and off diets several times a year, losing 20 pounds only to regain the weight in a few months.

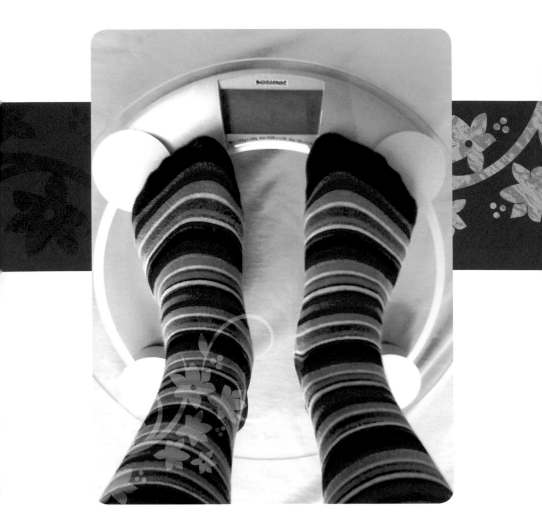

Destiny's eating habits weren't great, either. Although her mom cooked healthy dinners most nights, Destiny got pizza or cheeseburgers almost every day for lunch in the cafeteria, washing it all down with soda. She ate chips and ice cream at friends' houses while watching television after school, too. Her skinny friends ate the same way as she did, but they never seemed to gain any weight.

Destiny didn't play any sports. She didn't like Phys Ed because she was the slowest kid in her class. Every time she was picked last for a team or teased for breathing heavily, she hated exercise a little more. The only time she avoided teasing was when she didn't try as hard. If she didn't break a sweat, the other kids had less to tease her about.

Destiny channeled all of her frustration into her artwork. She filled sketchbook after sketchbook with drawings that expressed her feelings. Her art teacher, Ms. Silverman, consistently praised Destiny for the emotion in her charcoals and watercolors at school. Ms. Silverman even entered one of Destiny's charcoal drawings in a citywide contest sponsored by a local magazine.

Talk About It

- **Do you look like the women in your family? Are you happy about the way you look?**

- **Have you ever been teased at school? How did it make you feel?**

- **Which of Destiny's habits are healthy? Which of Destiny's habits are unhealthy? What can she do to change her unhealthy habits?**

One day after school, Destiny got a phone call. It was from the magazine. She had won first place in

the contest! The magazine was sending over a camera crew to take photographs of Destiny with her artwork. She was also invited to a special black-tie event for the contest winners. She was excited, but also a little worried. She didn't have anything fancy to wear to the party, and she didn't want to look fat in her magazine photos.

Destiny's mom was so happy when she heard the news. She also sensed Destiny's hesitation. "Don't worry, honey," she said. "We'll go to that new store in the mall. It has cool clothes for teens in your size. We'll get you new outfits for the photo shoot and the party."

That weekend, Destiny and her mom went shopping. Destiny's mom helped her pick out a gorgeous dress and some great jeans with a killer top. They chose new clothes that flattered her figure, rather than trying to hide it.

The photo shoot and the party both went really well. When Destiny saw her photo printed in the magazine, she thought she looked really pretty—and her artwork looked fantastic. At the party, no one teased her about her looks. Everyone wanted to talk to her about her art. She had a great discussion with one girl about her charcoal drawing. As the girl was leaving, she added, "And I love your dress! It looks so cute on you. Where did you get it?" Destiny grinned and told her. The compliment made her really happy.

Talk About It

- Have you ever won a competition? How did it make you feel?
- Have you ever tried a new style of clothes? How did the change make you feel?

After the party, Destiny noticed how great it felt when people paid attention to her for her talents. The competition made her realize that she didn't need to be limited—she could do anything.

And when she thought about it a little longer, she realized that she was tired of being teased and being the slowest kid in gym class. She thought, If I could win the art competition, why can't I get fit, too? She resolved to get healthy.

Destiny asked her mom to take her to her physician. Dr. Alice weighed Destiny and measured her height. She found that Destiny's weight was quite a bit higher than was healthy for her height. Dr. Alice also took Destiny's blood pressure, and it was high. And she took a blood test that showed Destiny had high cholesterol—the fatty stuff that can clog arteries.

And when she thought about it a little longer, she realized that she was tired of being teased and being the slowest kid in gym class.

Destiny had realized the teasing and tired parts of her life weren't great, but she wasn't expecting to hear she could actually get sick.

Dr. Alice explained, "High blood pressure and high cholesterol can put you at higher risk for getting dangerous diseases like heart disease and diabetes. We need to bring your blood pressure and cholesterol down."

Losing weight could help Destiny lower these risks. Together, Dr. Alice and Destiny put together a diet and exercise plan that Destiny thought she could really follow. Instead of pizza and cheeseburgers at school, Destiny would bring turkey sandwiches and fruit and buy milk from the cafeteria. She'd also cut back on the chips and ice cream at her friends' houses. Dr. Alice gave Destiny a bunch of ideas for healthy snacks, such as air-popped popcorn and yogurt with granola. She also gave Destiny some ideas for fun exercise, such as walking or biking with her friends.

Destiny laughed when Dr. Alice pointed these out. "You know, Destiny," Dr. Alice replied, "exercise doesn't have to mean gym class. It can mean doing things that are fun, and that just happen to get people moving." She even recommended a workout DVD that Destiny could do in her bedroom.

After the appointment, Destiny felt optimistic. She knew she was ready to try the new healthy steps.

Talk About It

- What do you think might happen if Destiny doesn't lose weight?

- Are you on any kind of healthy diet or exercise program?

The American Medical Association has found that more and more girls today are over the recommended weight for their height. That's not surprising, considering the average lifestyle for kids today. Kids are busier these days, and they are consuming a lot more calories than they did in the past. At the same time, kids exercise less than they once did. Most kids spend an average of three hours a day watching television and doing other seated activities.

Being overweight can be a constant struggle, especially if your friends are thin and all you see are images of tiny women in your favorite magazines and television shows. Remember that you don't need to be a size zero to be beautiful. Everybody is different, and some bodies are naturally larger than others. There is no ideal weight or body shape! You *do* need to be healthy, though, which means eating the right balance of foods and getting plenty of physical activity—no matter what your size.

Get Healthy

1. If you hate sports, try another kind of activity. Walking, dancing, and swimming all count as aerobic exercise. Every girl needs exercise, no matter what her weight is!

2. Try eating little healthy snacks throughout the day. They will rev up your metabolism and keep you from feeling hungry. Grapes, carrot sticks, whole-wheat crackers, and low-fat cheese all make great munchies.

3. Don't tease kids who are overweight. Being overweight does not mean that a person is lazy or has no self-control.

4. Don't obsess about the scale. Puberty causes girls to put on weight—this is normal. Ask your doctor if your weight is healthy, and get his or her advice for ways to eat right and get fit.

The Last Word from Stephanie

Being overweight can make adolescence tough. In the long term, this can also put you at greater risk for disease. It's important to stay healthy by eating right and getting enough exercise. Get all the help you can find—from your doctor, your friends, and your family. Never stop believing in yourself. Remember that you are a beautiful person both inside and out, and you can get healthy and maintain your healthy weight.

2

Too Sweet

Being overweight can have some serious health consequences. Diabetes is one possible result. As more kids are becoming overweight, health experts are noting a jump in the number of diabetes cases among tweens and teens.

Diabetes is a disease that affects insulin, a hormone your pancreas makes. Normally, insulin is released when you eat. It helps your body turn the sugars from food into energy. For people with diabetes, their body either doesn't produce enough insulin, or it doesn't use insulin effectively.

Some people are born with this condition. This is called type 1 diabetes.

When people are overweight, often their body doesn't use insulin correctly. This is called type 2 diabetes. As a result, the level of sugar in the blood gets higher and higher. Having a lot of sugar in your blood puts a big strain on your body. Your risk of getting type 2 diabetes is also linked to genes, race, a sedentary lifestyle, age, and certain medications.

Diabetes is a sneaky disease. Because its symptoms are sometimes not obvious, many kids who have diabetes don't realize they're sick.

When you have a disease like diabetes, things you never thought about before become challenges. You have to see the doctor more often and test your blood sugar many times each day. You also may have to miss out on some of your favorite activities because you don't feel well.

Diabetes is a sneaky disease. Because its symptoms are sometimes not obvious, many kids who have diabetes don't realize they're sick. When Sherri started feeling bad, diabetes was the last thing she expected to hear from her doctor.

Sherri's Story

Sherri loved chocolate. She also loved cookies, cake, ice cream, and doughnuts. If there was anything sweet within a one-mile radius, Sherri could sniff it out.

She was completely psyched when her birthday rolled around. That meant birthday cake *and* ice cream! Her parents were throwing her a party at her favorite Italian restaurant. Sherri's best friends, Joely and Mindy, were coming.

Her mom had ironed Sherri's favorite dress. All Sherri needed to do was put it on and fix her makeup, and they could leave for the restaurant. Oh, and she had to go to the bathroom again. It seemed like she always had to use the bathroom these days—in the middle of class, during soccer practice, or right as the school assembly was starting. "I'm probably drinking too much soda," Sherri thought to herself.

As excited as she was, once she got to the party Sherri didn't feel very well. She was really tired, even though she'd slept until ten o'clock that morning. And she felt sick to her stomach—so sick, in fact, that even the chocolate birthday cake with buttercream icing didn't look appealing. Her discomfort must have showed, because her mom, Joely, and Mindy kept asking what was wrong. Sherri just smiled and pretended everything was okay.

Talk About It

- Should Sherri have told her mother that she wasn't feeling well?
- Have you ever felt sick and kept it to yourself?

The next day was Saturday, and Sherri's parents wanted to take her to her favorite amusement park. Sherri could barely get out of bed. They didn't push her to go, but when she was still feeling awful on Monday, her mother insisted they go to her doctor for a checkup.

At the doctor's office, Sherri had to step on the scale and get weighed. All of the cookies, cake, and candy she'd been eating had caught up with her. She was officially overweight. The nurse took samples of Sherri's blood and urine and left the room. Sherri waited, dreading the lecture on dieting she was sure she'd get from her doctor. But when the doctor came into the room, he said something Sherri had never expected to hear: Sherri had diabetes.

As the doctor went through the list of health risks from having diabetes—heart disease, kidney disease, blindness, and nerve damage—Sherri's face turned white. This couldn't be happening to her! She was too young to have diabetes!

Talk About It

- **How do you think Sherri felt when she heard she had diabetes?**

- **What would you do if you learned you had diabetes?**

- **Do you have a serious health condition? If so, how did you react when you found out about it?**

The doctor explained that Sherri would have to check her blood sugar every day—sometimes more than once a day. That meant pricking her finger with a needle. Sherri absolutely hated needles. How was she going to stick herself with one every single day?

Then Sherri heard the words she dreaded most: she had to cut most of the sugar out of her diet.

A few days later, Sherri met with a nutritionist who put her on a diet. The diet required her to eat smaller portions, more fruits, vegetables, and lean meats, and lots of whole grains. Then, Sherri heard

the words she dreaded most: she had to cut most of the sugar out of her diet. No more cookies? No more candy bars? Life as she knew it was over!

Talk About It

- Do you listen to your doctor when he or she gives you advice?

- Have you ever had to make a big change to your diet?

- What might happen if Sherri keeps eating the way she used to eat?

Sherri felt miserable. No more Halloween candy. No more birthday cake. No more fun.

It wasn't like Sherri had a choice, though. She had to follow her doctor's orders if she wanted to avoid all those terrible diabetes complications. So, she tested her blood sugar every day, watched her diet, and started jogging in her neighborhood to control her weight.

After a couple of weeks, she started to feel better. She lost some weight, stopped feeling tired all the time, and no longer had to make constant runs for the bathroom.

At her next doctor's visit, the nurse tested her blood sugar again. The levels were way down! Then, the doctor gave her the best news: by controlling her diet and keeping her weight in check, Sherri could actually make her diabetes go away. She'd never be totally off the hook—she'd have to watch her blood sugar for the rest of her life—but she could be diabetes-free.

Sherri knew she would always miss the sweets—they were so hard to resist—but she learned that she could have a little bit of sugar once in a while. She found a few different kinds of sugar-free cookies and candies to help satisfy her sweet tooth. She also discovered that there was a big upside to dieting and working out. Losing weight meant Sherri needed to buy a brand-new wardrobe—and *that* was pretty sweet.

Learning that you have a serious disease such as diabetes can be really difficult. You already have a million things to worry about every day, and checking your blood sugar is just one more thing to add to your to-do list.

Using a team approach can really help kids with diabetes manage their disease. Parents can become part of the team by buying foods and preparing meals that fit with a diabetes diet. Friends can be part of the team by being understanding and offering encouragement. The principal, teachers, and school nurse can be part of the team by making sure that the school environment is safe and healthy.

It's also important to get in tune with your body and watch for the warning signs of diabetes, such as feeling cold or tired, or having to go to the bathroom more often than usual. Report any of these signs to your doctor right away.

Although some people are more likely to contract diabetes than others, if you watch your diet, exercise regularly, and don't overload on sweets, you can reduce your risk.

Get Healthy

1. Even if you don't have diabetes, it's a good idea to limit sweets. Avoid soda and don't eat more than one or two desserts a week.

2. Fill up on low-fat, healthy foods so you don't crave sweets as much.

3. Exercise for at least 60 minutes each day. If you have diabetes, check your blood sugar level before and after you exercise.

4. Always follow your doctor's advice, whether it's about taking medicine, exercising, or watching your diet.

The Last Word from Stephanie

Having diabetes doesn't mean you need to stop eating all of your favorite foods or participating in the activities you love. It won't suddenly turn you into a new person or cause you to act any differently than your friends. Diabetes doesn't define you—you are exactly the same person inside. Having diabetes does mean you will need to make a few adjustments to your life. Eat right, exercise daily, test your blood sugar regularly, and take any medication your doctor prescribes. If you closely follow the advice of your doctor, dietitian, and parents, you can keep your diabetes under control.

3

She's Nuts

Your immune system is your body's best defense. It's like an inner shield, protecting you from diseases that could make you really sick. Usually, the immune system works pretty well. Sometimes, though, it goes haywire and starts attacking when there's no real threat.

Allergies are an example of the immune system malfunctioning. In the case of food allergies, the body mistakenly sees a type of food—such as shrimp, peanuts, or milk—as a danger and launches an attack. The body produces chemicals to defend it against the food. These chemicals cause symptoms including rashes, a swollen tongue, or wheezing.

Sometimes, a food allergy is so severe that a person can have a reaction just from being in the same room with the food. Certain people are so allergic to a food that they may die if they eat it. Brittany has a severe allergy to peanuts. She's had to avoid them her whole life, and it hasn't been easy.

Brittany's Story

Brittany despised Halloween. She had hated the holiday ever since she was three years old and her mother had dressed her up in a Cinderella costume with glass slippers. It wasn't that she didn't like the costume, or the trick-or-treating. She just knew that every Halloween she had to endure the same ritual—her mother examining every single piece of candy, cutting each one open and scouring the label to make sure it didn't contain any trace of peanuts.

That Halloween when she was three, after taking her very first bite of a delicious candy bar, Brittany's lips swelled up. Her tongue grew so big that it filled her mouth, and she could barely

Certain people are so allergic to a food that they may die if they eat it.

breathe. Her parents rushed her to the hospital, and she had to spend the rest of her Halloween night in the emergency room.

From then on, Brittany lived in a peanut-free zone. No snacks with peanuts in them and definitely no peanut butter sandwiches. Because of

Brittany, her entire school was also a peanut-free zone, a fact that her friends constantly harassed her about. "Awww, man!" Marcus complained. "I have to eat bologna sandwiches every day because of you!"

Talk About It

- **How do you think being allergic to peanuts makes Brittany feel?**
- **Do you have any food allergies? Do your friends give you a hard time about it?**
- **Do you know anyone who has a food allergy? Do you treat that person differently because of his or her allergy?**

Even though Brittany had decided she was too old for trick-or-treating, Halloween still reminded her of how different she was from everyone else. Every year, her school had a costume parade, followed by a big Halloween bash in the gym. And every year, Brittany was banished to her guidance counselor's office because there was candy at the party. So many different candy bars contained peanuts, or traces of peanuts, that her mother was terrified Brittany would have an allergic reaction.

She did get to go to the parade, though. When it was time to start, everyone lined up outside the gym to march around the soccer field. Brittany was dressed

as a vampire, with a long black velvet cape and black-lined eyes and lips. She had to admit she looked good. A few of the boys in her class seemed to agree, because they kept smiling at her and whispering to each other. Maybe this Halloween wouldn't be so bad after all, she thought. Her mood brightened.

They marched around the soccer field—zombies, pop stars, presidents, and punks. Then, it was time to go to the gym. Brittany was feeling so pumped from the parade that she decided this year, there was no way she was missing the party. She managed to sneak into the gym without getting spotted by Ms. Floyd, the guidance counselor.

Talk About It

- **Do you think it's fair that Brittany is left out while her classmates celebrate?**
- **Do you agree with Brittany's decision to go to the party?**
- **How would you feel if you couldn't participate in a school event with all of your friends?**

Inside the gym, Brittany and her friends Lisbeth, Desiree, and Sierra hung out by the bleachers, drinking punch and chatting about everyone's costumes. Desiree handed each of them some candy bars she had taken from the snack table.

Brittany bit into her candy bar. It was so chocolatey and delicious. She chewed, and swallowed. It was so good!

A few seconds later, Brittany started to feel weird. Her lips were somehow not her lips anymore.

They were like two huge balloons attached to her face. Desiree looked at her strangely. "Girl, are you okay?" she asked. Brittany couldn't answer. Her tongue was suddenly huge. It seemed to fill her entire mouth.

Brittany mumbled what sounded like, "Wr dr nts in du cndee?" Her friends looked at her blankly. "Nuts!" she

Brittany couldn't answer. Her tongue was suddenly huge. It seemed to fill her entire mouth.

managed to yell through swollen lips. Desiree clapped a hand over her mouth. "Oh my gosh, I'm so sorry! There were *nuts* in the candy bars!" she exclaimed. Desiree went running for help.

Brittany couldn't breathe. Her throat was squeezing closed. Oh no, not here, she thought. I can't be having an allergic reaction in front of the entire school! But she *was* having a reaction, and she was starting to lose consciousness. The last thing she saw before she fainted was the nurse running toward her with a needle.

Talk About It

- **How do you think Brittany felt about having an allergic reaction in front of her classmates?**

- **Have you ever had an allergic reaction at school? How did you explain what happened to your classmates?**

After the nurse had given her a shot of epinephrine, Brittany's throat opened enough so she could breathe again. As she listened to the ambulance siren getting closer, she realized that she had just fainted in front of the entire school. Brittany wanted to cry. It was the most embarrassing day of her life. And how was she going to tell her mom?

If you have a food allergy, you may feel like the only one who has to avoid certain foods, but you're not alone. About 3 million kids in the United States have food allergies, and that number is rising. Most of them are allergic to foods such as milk, eggs, peanuts, shellfish, soy, or wheat. Sometimes people are allergic to more than one food, which makes eating even more challenging.

Food allergies are different for everyone. While some people get a mild rash, others may actually die if they're exposed to the food. That's why you should see an allergy specialist if you ever have a reaction to food. The doctor can test a tiny amount of different foods on your skin to look for signs of an allergic reaction.

Though there isn't a cure for food allergies, many kids do grow out of them eventually. In the meantime, it's really important if you do have an allergy to avoid the food that triggers your reaction, especially if your allergy is severe.

Get Healthy

1. Read food labels carefully. Some products are made in factories that also process the food that gives you an allergic reaction.

2. When you eat at a restaurant, don't just read the menu. Tell your server that you have

an allergy, and ask him or her to make sure your meal doesn't contain that ingredient.

3. Make sure your principal, teachers, and classmates know that you have a food allergy. Never share food with other kids at your school.

4. If you have a severe allergy, always carry an epinephrine pen (EpiPen) with you in case you have a reaction. Wear a medical alert bracelet or necklace to let other people know you have an allergy.

The Last Word from Stephanie

Food allergies can affect not only the kids who have them, but also everyone around them. So many kids are allergic to foods that many schools have special policies banning foods that are big allergy triggers. If your school doesn't let you eat peanuts or peanut butter sandwiches because one of your classmates has an allergy, you might be annoyed. Understand that it's not your classmate's fault. That person has to think about everything he or she eats, which isn't easy. Try to understand how she feels, and make sure you follow your school's dietary rules so your friend never has a reaction like Brittany did.

4

Dairy Girl

Have you ever eaten a certain type of food and then felt sick to your stomach afterward? You may be intolerant to that food. Food intolerance is a little like a food allergy, except the immune system isn't reacting to the food—the digestive system is.

With food intolerance, chemicals, bacteria, or other substances in the food irritate the digestive system. In other cases, the body can't break down the food well enough to digest it. A lot of people are sensitive to at least one type of food. Some people don't feel sick unless they eat a lot of the food that bothers them. Other people start feeling bad after just a few bites.

Usually, food intolerance isn't serious. It can be really embarrassing, though, because the symptoms are pretty gross (such as vomiting, gas, or diarrhea). Those symptoms can be especially humiliating if they happen while you're at school.

Megan's Story

May 5 was the annual ice cream party at Harold Seaver Middle School. As a reward for the students' hard work all year, the ice cream truck rolled into the parking lot and the students were treated to big sundaes with as many toppings as they could fit in their bowls.

By the end of fifth period, the classrooms were already buzzing. Everyone was looking forward to the upcoming

Food intolerance is a little like a food allergy, except that the immune system isn't reacting to the food—the digestive system is.

treat. When the bell rang, there was a run for the door, and everyone got in line beside the ice cream truck.

Megan and her friend Gabriela knew the routine and they went quickly to the front of the line. While they waited, they started planning their sundaes. "I'm having chocolate ripple ice cream with caramel sauce, chocolate chips, and whipped cream," Gabriela announced.

"I'm all about the mint chip and hot fudge with sprinkles," Megan replied.

Then, a little voice in Megan's mind started to whisper. "Remember the last time you ate ice cream..." it warned, and then faded away. Megan brushed it aside. So she was a little sensitive to dairy. Sometimes, it upset her stomach, but that was only when she ate a lot of it. A couple of ice cream scoops wouldn't hurt.

When they got to the truck's counter, the girls placed their orders. They walked away piling heaping spoonfuls of ice cream and toppings into their mouths.

Talk About It

- **Should Megan have listened to the inner voice that warned her not to eat ice cream?**

- **Are you sensitive to any foods?**

After the party was over, it was time to go back to class. Gabriela and Megan both had science sixth period with Mr. Fishman. They sat down in their seats and got out their notebooks and pens as Mr. Fishman started to describe the lesson for the day.

Fifteen minutes had gone by when Megan suddenly didn't feel so good. She was nauseated and her stomach was gurgling. Hearing Mr. Fishman talk about frog hearts and intestines wasn't helping.

Megan's stomach rumbled so loudly that a couple of kids turned to stare at her. A few seconds later,

unable to control herself, she let out a long, quiet fart. It sounded like air rushing out of a punctured tire. She hoped no one had heard, but the boy sitting in front of her turned around and snickered. Gabriela leaned over and whispered, "What's the matter?"

"Lactose intolerance!" Megan moaned.

The gurgling in her stomach was getting worse. A cold sweat broke out on Megan's forehead. She knew what was coming next. She had to get out of the classroom—quickly. Her hand shot up in the air. "Mr. Fishman, may I please go to the bathroom?" she asked. Megan heard a few muffled giggles from behind her as she ran out of the room.

Talk About It

- **Have you ever felt sick and had to leave the classroom? Were you embarrassed about it?**

- **How do you feel about the way Megan's classmates reacted?**

- **What do you think Megan should say when she gets back to class?**

Thankfully, the bathroom was empty. Sitting in the stall, her stomach raging, reminded Megan how awful it was to be lactose intolerant. Her body didn't have the right chemical to digest lactose—a substance in milk and other dairy products—so whenever she ate too much dairy, she got sick.

When it happened, it was really gross. She had gas, bloating, and really bad diarrhea. Not the things

she wanted to happen at school. The noises her body was making were disgusting. The smell was even worse.

Just then, the door swung open. She could hear the sounds of laughter as Melinda and her girl posse walked in. "Oh no, anyone but them!" Megan thought. Melinda and her crew were the most popular group of girls in the school, and they weren't known for their kindness. Megan tried her best to silence her raging stomach, but her body wouldn't obey.

"So I told him, if you want to come to my birthday party, you have to bring me a really amazing gift," Megan could hear Melinda announce on her way into the bathroom. Then there was a long pause. "What is that smell? Gross!" Megan couldn't help herself—just

Megan wanted to crawl under the floor and disappear. She swore she'd *never* eat ice cream again.

then she let out a loud fart. She could hear the girls giggling. "C'mon girls, let's use the bathroom on the second floor. This one is *totally* polluted," said Melinda, and the entire group of girls left the bathroom with a chorus of "Ewwws."

After a few minutes, Megan's stomach started feeling better. Mercifully, the bathroom stayed pretty empty, except for the one sixth grader who walked in while Megan was washing her hands. The girl shot Megan the evil eye after taking one sniff of the air.

In utter humiliation, Megan slunk back to her science class. Everyone was gathering up their books and getting ready to leave. They all stared at her. "Did you take a big dump?" Scott chortled. Megan wanted to crawl under the floor and disappear. She swore she'd *never* eat ice cream again.

Talk About It

- How do you think it made Megan feel to have a lactose intolerance attack in class?

- How would you have felt if that had happened to you?

Ask Dr. Robyn

A lot of kids are sensitive to dairy products or other types of foods. When your body can't absorb certain foods, they just sit in your gut, where they can cause bloating, gas, and diarrhea. It can be really embarrassing to have to run to the bathroom in the middle of school because your stomach is revolting against something you ate.

Food intolerance can't be cured, but there are ways to make it better. First, visit your doctor for tests to make sure that another health condition isn't causing your symptoms. Your doctor can find out exactly which food or foods are making you sick. Then you can try to avoid or limit those foods whenever possible. A dietitian can help you choose foods that won't trigger your symptoms.

People with lactose intolerance can take special medicines that help the body break down the sugar (lactose) in milk. Some kinds of milk and other dairy products come in lactose-free varieties.

Get Healthy

1. If you think you have food intolerance, keep a diary. Write down everything you eat, at what time, and how it made you feel. Take the diary to your doctor, who can use it to

figure out which type of food is making you feel sick.

2. If you're lactose intolerant and love milk and ice cream, there are special types of pills and dairy products that can help you digest those foods more easily.

3. Always read food labels and ask what ingredients are in your meals at restaurants so you don't get sick.

The Last Word from Stephanie

Having food intolerance can be really embarrassing, especially if it happens in front of your friends and schoolmates. Stomach problems such as passing gas, vomiting, and having diarrhea are considered disgusting—even though they're just natural body functions that happen to everyone. When you're faced with an embarrassing situation at school, you may feel as though you want to disappear, just like Megan. One great way to get out of a humiliating experience like Megan's is with humor. Sometimes, if you can make a joke about the situation, your friends will laugh with you, instead of at you. If it's your friend who has the food intolerance, try to be sensitive to her feelings. Imagine how you would feel in the same situation and how you would want your friend to react.

5

Wheezy Girl

Have you ever felt short of breath? You may have started breathing heavily after you ran very fast or exercised at high intensity. People who have asthma experience that same kind of feeling, but not only when they are exercising. They may have trouble breathing after smelling perfume, petting a dog, or being near tobacco smoke.

Asthma is a disease that affects the airways—the tubes that carry oxygen to and from the lungs so you can breathe. In people who have asthma, the airways swell and narrow so less air gets into the lungs.

Anyone who has ever had an asthma attack knows it can be scary. Your chest feels really tight, like someone is pressing down on it. You have to work extra hard just to get enough air into your lungs. It may feel as though you can't breathe.

If your friends don't know anything about asthma, they may have a hard time understanding why you're wheezing and coughing. They might be afraid or not know how to help you. People who don't know you well might even be mean and make fun of your symptoms instead of trying to help.

Tammi's Story

It had only been three months since Tammi and her family had moved from San Diego to Chicago. When she arrived at her new school, she was terrified she'd be branded "the new girl." Tammi thought no one would like her. She imagined having to sit alone at lunch every day.

Surprisingly, her worst fears didn't materialize. There she was, seated at the coolest table in the cafeteria, surrounded by the most popular girls at school. How amazing was that? To make the situation even more amazing, Laura, the head cheerleader, was now her best friend. As if to confirm their friendship, Laura leaned over and gave Tammi a big hug. "I'm so glad you moved here," she said.

In people who have asthma, the airways swell and narrow so less air gets into the lungs.

"Me too," Tammi replied.

After lunch was gym class—Tammi's favorite time of the day. She'd always been good at sports. At her old school, she'd played basketball, soccer, and tennis.

At the beginning of gym class, Tammi and her friends lined up underneath the basketball hoop so the coach could take attendance. Then, it was time to warm up with a stretch and a jog around the gym.

As she stretched, Tammi suddenly realized that she'd forgotten to use her asthma inhaler that morning. She'd had asthma since she was five years old, so carrying an inhaler was second nature to her. She always used it before gym because exercise could trigger her asthma symptoms. This morning, Tammi and Laura had been on the phone debating whether they should wear their matching jeans, and Tammi had been so distracted she'd left her inhaler sitting on the kitchen table at home.

Talk About It

- How would you feel if you had to carry an inhaler—or any other medicine—with you all the time?

- Have you ever forgotten to take medicine that you really needed? What happened?

- Do you think Tammi should have had a better system for remembering her inhaler?

Please don't let me have an asthma attack . . . please don't let me have an asthma attack, Tammi repeated over and over in her head to the rhythm of her running feet. No one at her new school knew she had asthma. She'd hidden it well, taking her medication every morning before school and sneaking into the bathroom to use her inhaler whenever she felt her chest start to tighten.

Tammi felt she had to keep her asthma a secret because at her last school, when the kids had found out, they had constantly teased her about it. "Hey, Wheezy!" Angelica used to call out from behind her when she walked down the hall. Then Angelica would mimic Tammi's forced breathing, her blonde ponytail bobbing up and down as she gasped for air. All of Angelica's friends would crack up laughing.

Tammi was determined not to let that happen at her new school. At this school, she was Tammi, not "Wheezy." For once in her life, she was popular.

But it *was* happening. As she ran, Tammi could feel the telltale pressure building in her chest. Her breaths were coming faster and shallower.

Talk About It

- What should Tammi have done when she started to have an asthma attack?

- Do you think Tammi's friends will stop liking her if they find out she has asthma?

- Do you know anyone who has asthma? How do you feel about that person?

There was no way to hide it. By now, everyone in class had noticed something was wrong with Tammi, who stood in the middle of the gym, coughing, wheezing, and gasping for air. Coach Jones walked over, a concerned look on her face.

Laura also walked over. "This is it," Tammi thought miserably. "I'm done being one of the popular girls."

Laura didn't laugh at her, though. She didn't even snicker. Her face was completely serious. "Come with me—quick," she ordered.

Tammi walked with Laura all the way to the school nurse's office, their coach just a few paces behind. Laura was in charge the whole time. "You have an extra inhaler in Nurse Johnson's office, right?" she asked. Tammi paused, and then nodded. She had completely forgotten that she had left an extra inhaler with the school nurse in case of an emergency.

There was no way to hide it. By now, everyone in class had noticed something was wrong with Tammi, who stood in the middle of the gym, coughing, wheezing, and gasping for air.

By the time they reached the nurse's office, Tammi could barely breathe. Laura led her into the room and told the nurse, "We need Tammi Jenkin's inhaler!" The nurse opened a drawer and pulled out Tammi's inhaler. She handed it to Tammi, who leaned her head back, pressed down on the inhaler to release the medicine, and breathed in slowly for a few seconds.

A few minutes later, when she was finally able to breathe more freely, Tammi looked at Laura gratefully.

"Thanks so much for not laughing at me," she said. "And thanks for helping me out. How did you know what to do?"

Laura smiled as she reached into the nurse's drawer and pulled out an inhaler identical to Tammi's, marked with her own name. "You could say I've had some experience," she replied.

Talk About It

- How do you think Tammi felt when she learned Laura also had asthma?

- Have you ever gotten closer to someone at school because you shared a similar problem?

Unfortunately, there's no cure for asthma. There are ways to live with it, though. Medicine can reduce or totally relieve symptoms, allowing kids with asthma to do all of the things they love—including playing sports.

Asthma is nothing to be embarrassed about—there are probably several kids in your class with the condition. If you prefer not to take medication during school hours, you can take it in the morning and at night. If you have asthma, it's a good idea to carry an inhaler or keep one in the school nurse's office. Check it often to make sure it still has enough medicine.

Also, get to know what triggers your asthma symptoms. For some people the trigger is dust. For others, it's a friend's pet. Try to avoid anything that causes you to wheeze and have trouble breathing. A device called a peak flow meter can help measure how well your lungs are working, and it may help you predict when you're about to have an asthma attack so you can take your medicine ahead of time.

Get Healthy

1. Don't smoke, and stay away from people who smoke. Smoke can cause asthma and trigger attacks in people who already have the condition. Also avoid allergens such as

pets and pollen because these can lead to asthma symptoms.

2. Exercise regularly. Although exercise can cause asthma attacks in some people, it can also help prevent them by helping maintain a healthy weight. Getting fitter can help manage asthma and improve lung function.

3. If you have asthma, make sure to take your medicine just as your doctor prescribes. Keep an inhaler handy at all times.

4. A severe asthma attack is always an emergency. If you or a friend is having trouble breathing, get medical help right away.

The Last Word from Stephanie

Nobody wants to be known as the "girl with asthma," or "Wheezy," but that shouldn't force you to keep your asthma a secret. It can help to tell your friends and teachers you have asthma so they understand what's going on if you do have an attack. Never let asthma—or any other condition—stop you from being who you are or limiting what you can accomplish. Track-and-field star Jackie Joyner-Kersee and swimmer Amy Van Dyken both have asthma, but it didn't stop them from winning Olympic gold medals. You may need to take your medicine so you can perform at your peak, but you can still accomplish amazing things.

6

Girl on Wheels

Having any kind of difference, whether it's wearing braces or having bad acne, can make you feel like an outsider among your peers. When you have to use a wheelchair, you can feel as though you're living on another planet.

Kids who live with physical disabilities know they are different from other kids. They understand there are some things they just can't do, no matter how hard they try—such as running across a soccer field or jumping up to dunk a basketball.

They also know they are different because other kids remind them of it every single day. Kids can say hurtful things—

not necessarily because they want to be mean—but because they don't understand what it's like to have a disability. Some kids don't even have to speak. They can make a physically challenged person feel like an outsider just by passing them in the hallway without saying hi or not including them in a conversation. Kaitlyn was one of the girls everyone passed by. She didn't think anyone at school even knew her name.

Kaitlyn's Story

It was a Saturday afternoon, and Kaitlyn was spending it at the mall. She wasn't going there to hang out with the kids from school. Kaitlyn was going shopping with her mother.

Kaitlyn didn't have anything against her mom, who was actually very hip for a 40-year-old. They went to all the coolest stores and had lunch together. It was just that Kaitlyn would have loved to hang out in the food court with a big group of girls instead, drinking frozen lattes and gossiping about boys. There just weren't any girls to hang out with at the mall because Kaitlyn didn't have any friends.

Kids can say hurtful things—not necessarily because they want to be mean—but because they don't understand what it's like to have a disability.

Kaitlyn wasn't shy. In fact, she could start a conversation with anyone. It was just that no one wanted to be friends with the girl in the wheelchair.

Talk About It

- **What advice would you give Kaitlyn?**

- **Do you know anyone in your school who uses a wheelchair? Have you ever talked to him or her?**

Kaitlyn was born with cerebral palsy, which made it difficult for her to control the muscles in her body. Because the disease affected her legs, she had to use a wheelchair to get around.

When Kaitlyn was at school—or anywhere else, for that matter—the only thing everyone seemed to see was her wheelchair. At best, the other kids would look at her with sympathy and offer to open a door or help her with her books. At worst, they would laugh at the way she struggled with her locker, or would tease her about being drunk when she slurred her words. Cerebral palsy also affected the muscles around Kaitlyn's mouth.

Most of the time, everyone just ignored her. When Kaitlyn would wheel by a group of girls in her grade with a big smile on her face, they would look the other way. At lunch, she'd sit at the teachers' table in the cafeteria. After school, she'd go home alone, watching enviously as the other kids left in groups, on their way to a study session or a get-together at someone's house.

Talk About It

- **Have you ever been left out? How did it make you feel?**

- **When you see someone sitting alone at school, what do you do?**

On Monday, there was a special assembly at school. Kaitlyn was really nervous, because she was going to be in the show. Her wheelchair dance company was performing a piece that she had choreographed. Kaitlyn had to admit that she was a really good dancer and choreographer. She'd been performing for four years, and she'd won several awards in competitions. Kaitlyn had been rehearsing extra hard because she'd be performing in front of her classmates for the first time.

All of the students and teachers gathered in the auditorium and the lights dimmed. Kaitlyn waited behind the scenes for the music to start. When she heard her cue, she rolled onto the darkened stage. The spotlight hit her and Kaitlyn began to dance. She twirled. She whirled. She gracefully stretched her arms into the air. She and her dance partner, Max, met in the center of the stage. They held hands and spun each other around. Kaitlyn beamed. For those few minutes, it didn't matter that she couldn't walk. She could dance.

When the song ended, the whole auditorium was silent. Then everyone started to cheer. A couple of people screamed, "Yay, Kaitlyn!" It was incredible. She didn't think anyone at school actually knew her name.

After the show, the lights went back up and Kaitlyn's dance company held a question-and-answer session. One girl asked, "How did you learn to do those spins with your wheelchair?" Another student wanted to know if the company members ever wished they could dance for real. Kaitlyn answered, "We *are* dancing for real. We're just doing it in a different way."

Another student wanted to know if the company members ever wished they could dance for real. Kaitlyn answered, "We *are* dancing for real. We're just doing it in a different way."

Talk About It

- How do you think wheelchair dancing makes Kaitlyn feel?

- Do you participate in any activities that make you feel really good about yourself?

- Does anyone at school know what you're good at?

After she had said good-bye to the other dancers in her company, Kaitlyn headed back to class. Everyone was already in their classrooms, so the halls were pretty empty. Kaitlyn didn't mind, though. She was used to being alone.

When she wheeled in through the door of her classroom, something was definitely different. Instead of being ignored, Kaitlyn was suddenly the center of attention. Everyone turned to look at her. Lindsey, who had never so much as glanced in her direction, was beaming at her. "You are the most amazing dancer I have ever seen," she gushed. "I dance too, but I'm nowhere near that good. I had no idea you could dance in a wheelchair! Maybe we can get together and you can show me some of those cool moves!"

Kaitlyn grinned, basking in her classmates' sudden attention. They're interested in me, she thought. They want to get to know me!

Kids with disabilities often have to deal with loneliness and other emotional issues that can arise from being disabled. It can be hard to make friends. When someone is different, it can be hard for the people around him or her to know how to react or what to say. Some people can be fake-nice or condescending. Others can be really unkind.

It's important to remember that a physical disability only affects someone's body—not his or her mind or personality. The only difference between Kaitlyn and other girls is that she can't use her legs and her speech is slurred. She can still go to class, go shopping, and dance.

Understanding is a big part of acceptance. When you're unsure about a person's disability, it's okay to ask questions, as long as you ask them in a kind way. Knowing a little about a person who is disabled and being aware of his or her feelings can help both of you feel more comfortable around one another. And if you have a disability, consider ways you can help others see you for the amazing person you are.

Get Healthy

1. Always focus on your strengths, not your weaknesses. Think about what you can do and never let anything hold you back.

2. Never tease others for any reason, especially not for having a disability.

3. If there is a person at school who is in a
   wheelchair or has another type of disability,
   make an effort to talk to him or her. Don't
   be afraid to ask, in a polite way, about his or
   her disability and how he or she feels about
   it. Of course, don't forget to ask the person
   other questions that help you get to know
   who he or she is beyond the disability!

4. Find a community of people who are dealing with the same issues you are. That way,
   you'll always have a place where you can
   feel really comfortable.

The Last Word from Stephanie

Just because someone gets around on four
wheels instead of two legs doesn't mean she
is any different from you on the inside. Girls like
Kaitlyn want the same things you want—to do
well in school, to have friends they can hang out
with, and to feel accepted. The next time you
see someone in a wheelchair, take a minute to
stop and talk to her. Find out what kind of music
she likes. Ask what she does after school and
on the weekends. Once you get to know her,
you might find that the two of you are more
alike than you had imagined.

7

Slow Reader

For some kids, school comes easily. They can answer every question the teacher throws at them and they ace tests without even studying. Others can do well if they apply themselves and study hard. But for some kids, school is a constant struggle. No matter how hard they work, they just can't seem to get good grades.

These kids may have learning disabilities, which means their brains have more trouble than usual processing and understanding information. Some kinds of learning disabilities affect the ability to concentrate. Other learning disabilities make it harder to read or do math problems.

Dyslexia is one of the most common learning disabilities. People with dyslexia have trouble recognizing and reading words. When they look at a combination of letters, their brains don't correctly process the symbols to form words and sentences, so all they see is a confusing jumble.

Having a learning disability means you need to use different methods to study, do your homework, and take tests. It doesn't mean you're dumb.

Having a learning disability means you need to use different methods to study, do your homework, and take tests. It doesn't mean you're dumb. Nicole has spent her whole life trying to convince her classmates and teachers she's not stupid.

Nicole's Story

It was third period. English class. Otherwise known as the absolute worst time of the day. Nicole's feet shuffled down the hallway, moving as slowly as they could possibly go. She silently wished that a big sinkhole would open up under the school or a fire alarm would go off so that third period would be cancelled.

No such luck. When the third period buzzer rang, the school remained intact and there was no sign of sinkholes or fire anywhere.

Nicole slid into her seat. Not only did she have to endure English class, but today they were reading aloud from *The Diary of Anne Frank*. Nicole loved the story of the young Jewish girl who had to hide from the Nazis during World War II. She'd seen the movie and listened to the book on tape. She just dreaded the thought of having to read the book aloud to her class.

Talk About It

- **Why do you think Nicole was so upset about having to read aloud?**

- **Have you ever dreaded going to class? What was the reason?**

Miss Parker came in and started the class by handing back the essays everyone had written the week before. Nicole got a D, as usual. Bad grades were such a common occurrence for her that she barely blinked anymore when she got a D or an F. Yet, Nicole couldn't miss the disapproving look Miss Parker gave her when she handed back the graded essay.

When that minor humiliation was over, it was time for the major humiliation. "Nicole, why don't you start the reading for us," Miss Parker said. Nicole clutched her book. She glanced at her classmates and saw several snide grins in response.

Her hands shaking, Nicole opened the book. The words looked like a jumble. Nothing made sense. She started to read, tentatively. "Then . . . on the . . . ta . . . ta . . . table . . . there were . . . a bunch . . ."

A couple of the kids laughed. She heard someone whisper, "What a moron!"

"That's enough, Nicole. Thank you," Miss Parker interrupted. "Josh, please continue reading." She motioned to a boy sitting in the front of the class. Nicole's cheeks burned and tears welled up in her eyes.

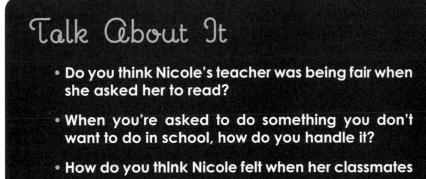

Talk About It

- **Do you think Nicole's teacher was being fair when she asked her to read?**

- **When you're asked to do something you don't want to do in school, how do you handle it?**

- **How do you think Nicole felt when her classmates laughed at her?**

Nicole tried not to let her experience in English class get to her, but she was still upset when she got home from school. Her mom asked what was bugging her. Usually she just said "nothing," but today she told her mom what had happened. "You've been struggling a lot in English, haven't you?" her mom replied. "I think it's time we took you to a specialist."

A few days later, they went to see three different specialists. Nicole's eye doctor tested her vision to make sure her eyesight wasn't affecting her reading; a psychologist gave her an IQ test to check her intelligence; and another expert evaluated her reading,

writing, and math skills. The verdict: Nicole was definitely not stupid. She had dyslexia.

The learning disabilities specialist explained that because of dyslexia, when Nicole looked at a sentence that read:

The girl went shopping at the mall.
Instead, she saw something like:

Thegi rlwe ntshop ping ath emall.

That was why she had struggled so hard to read and write. The specialist came up with a plan to help Nicole read better. Nicole's parents, teachers, and school guidance counselor were all going to be involved.

Nicole worked with a special teacher at school, who helped her adapt to her dyslexia by learning the sounds of letters—a technique called phonics. She also went to a learning center twice a week after school so she could catch up in reading and writing.

Talk About It

- **Have you ever had trouble in one of your subjects, such as reading or math?**

- **Have you ever needed extra academic help?**

- **How would you feel if you were told you had a learning disability?**

Nicole had to skip English class for a few weeks while she got extra help. Finally, she was doing well enough in her reading to go back to regular class. On her first day back, Nicole sat down in her old seat. Despite all of her hard work over the past few weeks, that same feeling of dread Nicole had experienced for years started to creep back in.

Despite all of her hard work over the past few weeks, that same feeling of dread Nicole had experienced for years started to creep back in.

Just her luck—they were reading aloud again. But this time, Nicole wasn't chosen first to read. She wasn't chosen second, or even third. In fact, Miss Parker skipped over her entirely.

Just when class was about to end, Miss Parker finally looked in her direction. "Nicole, would you like to read?" she asked kindly. Nicole paused. The memory of the other kids laughing at her was still vivid. Then she remembered how well she had been doing with her tutor. Tentatively, Nicole nodded.

She began to read, slowly at first, and then with more confidence. Nicole wasn't the best reader in the class, but she could finally hold her own. No one laughed this time. A couple of kids actually looked impressed. Nicole finished the paragraph and breathed a little sigh of relief. Maybe she didn't need a sinkhole after all.

Having a learning disability doesn't mean you're stupid. In fact, most kids with learning disabilities are of average or above-average intelligence. A learning disability also doesn't mean you can't learn. You just have to work harder to keep up with your classmates.

If you're struggling to read, write, or finish assignments on time, don't keep it a secret. Having a learning disability not only affects your schoolwork, but it can also be really hard on your self-esteem.

Talk to your parents and guidance counselor. They can have you tested to make sure it's not your eyesight or a problem with your nervous system that's making it difficult for you to learn. Once you know what's causing the problem, your parents, teachers, and counselors will work together to get you the extra assistance you need.

Learning disabilities don't go away—they last an entire lifetime. But with the right adjustments and teaching, people can overcome them and lead very successful lives.

Get Healthy

1. If reading and writing are difficult for you, there are other ways you can learn. Get books with large print, or listen to books on

tape. Record your classes instead of trying to take notes. Ask your teacher if you can dictate essays to someone rather than writing or typing them yourself.

2. Allow yourself a little more time to do your homework, and ask your teachers if you can have extra time to finish tests.

3. Set up a schedule for doing your homework each day. Do your work in a quiet area where there are no distractions.

4. Don't let your whole life revolve around school. Participate in after-school activities that you really enjoy, such as swimming, theater, or martial arts.

The Last Word from Stephanie

Thomas Edison was one of the greatest inventors of all time. If it hadn't been for him, lightbulbs, record players, and movies might never have existed. Thomas Edison was also dyslexic. Even though he had trouble reading, he was able to change the world. Edison's example proves that someone with a learning disability can succeed with hard work and perseverance. If you're struggling in school, it might feel like a major hurdle, but you can overcome it. Never let anyone call you stupid or make you think you're not worthwhile. Remember that you are smart, and with the right help, you're capable of doing anything you want to accomplish.

8

Four Eyes

There is an old expression that says "the eyes are the windows to the soul." That's a flowery way of saying your eyes can tell a lot about you. The saying may or may not be true, but your eyes are definitely your windows to the world. If they're not focusing clearly, you can have a really hard time seeing at school, while you're playing sports, or when you go to the movies.

Eye problems such as nearsightedness, farsightedness, or astigmatism are really common. Kids who have eye problems often need to wear glasses to help them see more clearly.

Some kids like wearing contact lenses better than glasses, making it hard to tell that they're wearing vision correction. However, contact lenses aren't right for everyone. Some people have eyes that are the wrong shape for contacts. Others aren't comfortable putting the lenses into their eyes. Hanna is afraid to get contact lenses, and she's been avoiding wearing her glasses. Her teachers have started to notice.

Hanna's Story

"Hanna, stop squinting!" Mrs. Marsh barked as Hanna stumbled over the math problems on the board. Hanna was trying to focus so hard that her eyes were nearly shut. Everyone in class giggled. "See me after class, please," Mrs. Marsh said after Hanna finally managed to come up with the right answer.

Hanna sank down in her seat. "Great, I'm being punished for not being able to see," she thought. Since school had begun a couple of months ago, Hanna had been squinting at everything—the chalkboard, the stage at school assemblies, and the movies, where her friends always wanted to sit in the back row.

Hanna was trying to focus so hard that her eyes were nearly shut.

Even though Mrs. Marsh had moved her closer to the front of the classroom, Hanna's vision was so bad that everything that wasn't right in front of her eyes was a total blur.

Hanna's mother had taken her to the eye doctor before school started. Dr. Lawsky had checked her vision, proclaimed that she was nearsighted, and prescribed a pair of glasses. Great—they made her look like an owl. At least, that's what her friends said when she wore her glasses the first day of school. One kid had actually hooted at her. Plus, when she played soccer the glasses kept slipping down her nose. Hanna couldn't score a goal when she was constantly pushing up her glasses.

After that, Hanna brought her glasses to school every day, but she left them in her book bag. She'd squint if she had to, but there was no way she was going to look like an owl.

Talk About It

- **Do you wear glasses? How do you feel about wearing them?**
- **Have you ever felt self-conscious about glasses, braces, or anything else you've had to wear?**
- **How do you think wearing glasses makes Hanna feel?**

When everyone had left the room after math class, Hanna walked up to Mrs. Marsh's desk. "Hanna, I think you need to wear glasses. You have to be able to see the board to do well in my class," Mrs. Marsh said. When Hanna explained why she didn't wear her

glasses, her teacher suggested, "Why don't you ask your parents about getting contact lenses? They'll help with your vision, and no one will have any idea you're wearing them."

"Great idea," Hanna replied with fake sincerity. The trouble was, Hanna was really squeamish. Just the thought of having to put something onto her eyeball made her feel woozy.

Still, it would be nice to be able to see clearly again without having to wear glasses. She decided it wouldn't hurt to ask her mom about contact lenses.

Hanna's mom took her back to Dr. Lawsky's office the following week. He checked her eyes again and

fitted her for contact lenses. Then, he showed Hanna how to put the lenses in her eyes. First, she washed her hands with soap and water. Then, she gently removed each lens from its case and rinsed it with contact lens solution. "So far, so good," Hanna thought.

While balancing a contact lens on one finger, Hanna gently pulled down on her right bottom eyelid as the eye doctor instructed. She moved the finger holding the lens closer and closer to her eye. The contact lens began to swim back and forth in her vision. Hanna started to feel so dizzy that she dropped the contact lens right on the floor. "I can't do this," she announced. "No way."

Talk About It

- **Why do you think putting in a contact lens bothers Hanna so much?**

- **Does anything make you feel squeamish, like the sight of blood or touching your eye?**

- **Do you think Hanna should give up on the idea of wearing contact lenses, or should she keep trying?**

Hanna was done. She was over contact lenses for good. Dr. Lawsky was persistent, though. "It takes time to get used to inserting contact lenses," he insisted. "Let's try again."

For the next hour, he patiently worked with Hanna. They went through each step very slowly, until Hanna was comfortable enough to move on to the next step. Finally, Hanna tried the entire sequence by herself.

When she called on Hanna to read a problem off the board, for the first time Hanna read it perfectly with absolutely no squinting.

Wash hands . . . rinse lens . . . insert in eye . . . She did it! Finally, she was able to put both contact lenses into her eyes. When Dr. Lawsky asked her to read the eye chart, she got every single line right—even the very bottom line.

Even though she had to give herself an extra half hour to get ready in the morning, Hanna wore her new contact lenses to school the next day. Her mom and Dr. Lawsky had both reassured her that inserting the lens would take less time as she became more practiced with them.

At school, none of Hanna's friends even noticed her contacts. Mrs. Marsh noticed, though. When she called on Hanna to read a problem off the board, Hanna read it perfectly with absolutely no squinting. As Hanna was walking out of class, Mrs. Marsh motioned for her to come over to her desk. "I'm guessing you paid a visit to the eye doctor," she said with a smile. Hanna nodded. "It's nice to see that you're not squinting anymore. Those frown lines aren't good for your complexion."

Hanna laughed and ran off to join her friends. They were going to the movies after school, and for the first time, Hanna didn't care if they sat in the back row.

Vision problems such as nearsightedness and farsightedness are really common in young people, so if you're squinting at the board or movie screen, you're definitely not the only one. There's no reason to squint, though, when there are so many options out there for improving your vision.

There are many fashionable options for glasses frames. Glasses don't have to make you look like an owl! If you don't like the idea of wearing glasses, your eye doctor may be able to fit you for contact lenses. These lenses can correct your vision almost invisibly. You'll need to keep them clean and make sure to take them out as often as your doctor instructs.

Even if you have perfect 20/20 vision today, it's important to take good care of your eyes and see your eye doctor regularly for checkups. That way, you'll make sure you can see clearly for years to come.

Get Healthy

1. The most important thing you can do for your vision is to get regular eye checkups. See an ophthalmologist at least once every two years, and more often if you're experiencing any vision trouble or have a family history of eye diseases.

2. If your doctor prescribes contact lenses, take good care of them. Wash your hands before handling your lenses. Clean both your contact lenses and the case with a sterile solution. Only wear your own contact lenses—never borrow anyone else's lenses.

3. Wear good sunglasses whenever you're outside. The sun's ultraviolet (UV) rays can damage your eyes and lead to future vision problems. Also, wear protective glasses whenever you work with chemicals in science class or do projects in shop class.

4. Try not to stare at the television, video games, or your computer screen for too long. Take breaks every few minutes to rest your eyes or look around the room.

The Last Word from Stephanie

I was very lucky to have had perfect vision throughout my childhood. Now that I'm older, I'm nearsighted. Without my glasses, I can't see things that are far away. I wear my glasses most of the time because it's such a relief to see the world clearly. You'll find that if you listen to your eye doctor and wear your glasses or contact lenses as prescribed, life will get much easier. Your eyes are so important—make sure you do everything to preserve your sight now, and you'll avoid a whole lot of vision problems down the road.

9

Tongue-Tied

Everyone stumbles over their words from time to time, especially when they get nervous. Have you ever given a speech in front of your class and found it difficult to get the right words out of your mouth in the right order?

People who stutter have trouble getting their words right much of the time. They may repeat certain sounds in words ("D-d-d-do you have a p-p-pencil?"), stretch out sounds ("Wwwwwhat do you mmmean?"), or stop completely in the middle of a sentence.

Many kids stutter when they're first learning how to speak. Sometimes the stuttering stops once a child becomes fluent in language. In other cases, the problem continues into middle school, high school, and even adulthood.

Kids who stutter are sometimes afraid to read aloud, raise their hands to answer questions in class, or get up and speak in front of their classmates. Brianna was absolutely terrified of public speaking—until her fear got in the way of an amazing opportunity.

Brianna's Story

Posters were going up all around the hallways of Redwood Middle School. "Vote for Karen Hannigan—School President!" and "Do you want ice cream in the cafeteria? Then vote for Billy Wallace on September 10!"

Brianna wanted to hang up her own campaign poster. She thought she'd make the perfect school president—she was smart,

Kids who stutter are sometimes afraid to read aloud, raise their hands to answer questions in class, or get up and speak in front of their classmates.

well organized, and she had great ideas. Then, Brianna thought about the debate she'd have to have with the other candidates, and the speech she'd have to give, and her dreams of becoming school president vanished.

Not everyone had given up on the idea of her running for school president, though. Brianna's homeroom teacher, Mr. Marks, called her over to his desk one morning before school started. "Brianna, why haven't I seen any of your campaign posters hanging up in the hallway? You have such great ideas on how to improve things around here," he said.

"I-I-I-I'm not running," she said softly.

"I think you'd make a tremendous school president," Mr. Marks replied. "Please let me know if you change your mind. I'd be happy to help you prepare your speech."

That whole day, Brianna thought about what Mr. Marks had said. He had a lot of confidence in her. The question was—did she have enough confidence in herself?

Talk About It

- **Would you be nervous about running for office at your school?**

- **Why do you think Brianna is so worried?**

- **If someone who stuttered was running for class president at your school, how would you react?**

The next day was the last chance to nominate students for school president. Brianna's best friend, Mercedes, tried to talk her into running. "C'mon, Brianna! I *so* want to be your campaign manager! Please let me nominate you!"

Mercedes begged and pleaded for a full 20 minutes before Brianna finally broke down and agreed to run. She dreaded the idea of giving a speech, but she really did want the job.

The two girls got right to work. They made posters, baked cookies and wrote Brianna's name across them in icing, and even printed a few T-shirts with Brianna's picture on them. During the entire next week, Mercedes spent every free second getting the word out about her best friend and what a great school president she would make.

Then, it was time for the debate. There were three candidates for school president—Brianna, Karen

Hannigan, and Billy Wallace—onstage in the auditorium. The debate moderator asked the first question: "What one thing would you do to make this school better?" Karen said something about promoting equality for everyone, and Billy wanted to put soda machines on every floor of the school. Then it was Brianna's turn. She leaned into the microphone, ready to wow everyone with her plan to raise money for new after-school activities, like digital photography and rock band.

"I-I-I-I'm B-B-B-Brianna," she began. She heard some muffled laughter from the audience. "M-m-m-my idea is to r-r-r-raise m-m-m-money for n-n-new a-a-after-school a-a-activities." She was so nervous that she couldn't get a single word out!

Talk About It

- How would you feel if you were in Brianna's place?

- Did you ever have to get up and speak in front of your class? What did you do?

- Have you ever been teased because of something you said, or the way you said it?

The debate was an utter disaster. There was no way Brianna was going to win for school president after that performance, and she told Mercedes as much when they met at lunch. "So you stuttered a little. You had great ideas," Mercedes insisted. Brianna was ready to throw in the towel, but her friend refused to let her give up.

To prepare for her upcoming speech, Brianna visited her speech therapist. The therapist worked with her on relaxation techniques, and showed her how to speak more slowly while breathing deeply. The therapist also suggested playing music in the background while Brianna spoke, because she said sometimes music helps people stop stuttering.

She breathed deeply—in and out—just as her speech therapist had recommended. When it was her time to speak, she stepped confidently to the microphone.

Brianna also took up Mr. Marks on his offer to help her with her speech. She went to his classroom every day after school to practice. She read the speech with him over and over again, until she knew it by heart. Mr. Marks announced, "Good job! I think you're ready to go on."

When the school had assembled again in the auditorium a couple of days later, Brianna waited onstage patiently for her turn at the podium. She breathed deeply—in and out—just as her speech therapist had recommended. When it was her time to speak, she stepped confidently to the microphone.

"H-h-hey! D-d-do y-y-you know wh-wh-where I-I-I c-c-can learn to t-t-t-alk like y-y-you?" a boy yelled

from the front row. Brianna froze, her cheeks turning bright pink. "That's enough!" said Principal Brown.

Brianna wanted to turn and run off the stage, but she wasn't about to give up after all the hard work she had put into rehearsing for this speech. She took a deep breath and began to speak slowly and deliberately. "M-m-my name is Brianna Davis, and I want to be your school president. W-w-w-what am I going to do for this school?" She paused. Behind her, Mercedes pressed a button on the tape recorder and the sounds of "We Will Rock You" filled the auditorium.

Over the music, Brianna explained to the students how she was going to work to get them the best after-school programs in the state. She was so into her speech that she hardly stuttered once. "Once we get our rock band program up and running, Redwood Middle School will really . . ." "Rock you!" the song finished.

The auditorium went wild. Everyone cheered. As Brianna walked off the stage, Mercedes ran up to her with her hand extended. "I just wanted to be the first to shake hands with our new school president!" she said.

Talk About It

- Why do you think Brianna's speech was such a great success?

- Is there anything that you have worked really hard to achieve? What was it?

Ask Dr. Robyn

Stuttering does not mean that you are stupid or slow. Stuttering is simply an interruption in the flow of speech. Typically, it happens when there's a problem with the way the brain's messages get to the muscles and body parts needed for speaking.

Most kids grow out of stuttering eventually, but in the meantime, getting help from a professional can make their lives a lot easier. There are many treatments for stuttering. A speech and language specialist (called a speech pathologist) can teach those who stutter how to relax, speak more slowly, and control their breathing. Treatment can really improve self-esteem in kids who stutter and help them perform better in school.

If you know someone who stutters, try to be understanding. See the problem from her perspective. She is trying her best to get the words out, and if you roll your eyes or tap your foot, she is only going to get more flustered. Don't try to correct her or finish her sentences. Wait patiently until she is finished speaking and respond as you would to any conversation.

Get Healthy

1. If you stutter, or just get nervous when you speak, relax and slow down. Try breathing

deeply, which can sometimes help the words flow more easily.

2. Practice having conversations with your parents and friends when you're not stressed out or worried about getting your words right.

3. Imagine the letters and words in your head before you begin speaking.

4. When giving a speech, start with a funny story. It can help break the ice and make you less nervous about speaking in front of a group.

The Last Word from Stephanie

When James Earl Jones was a boy, he stuttered so badly that he wouldn't say more than a few words at a time, even to his family. Today, he is one of the most famous actors and voice-over talents in Hollywood. You've probably heard his voice in movies such as *The Lion King* and the *Star Wars* series (he was the voice of Darth Vader). Just like many kids, Jones was able to overcome his stutter. If you have difficulty getting the words right—whether you stutter or you're just nervous speaking in front of other people—with a little bit of determination and a lot of belief in yourself, you can become a better, more confident speaker.

A Second Look

When I was in school, I didn't wear glasses, use a wheelchair, or have a weight problem. That didn't mean I was perfect, though. I was terribly shy. I could barely look up at the other kids when I walked through the halls at school, and my classmates used to tease me horribly.

Adults often like to say, "I wish I had known then what I know now." And it's true: growing up gave me an entirely new perspective on life. A few years made a big difference in my life—as it probably will in yours, too.

For now, though, being different likely isn't easy, especially considering that this is the time in your life when all you want to do is fit in. Just as I experienced when I was in school, kids can be really cruel. When you're already feeling hyperconscious about yourself, hearing taunts like "fatty" or "four eyes" can only make you feel worse.

It's important to remember that everyone is unique. One person may be really tall while another is short; one can be stocky while another is lanky. Try to change your perspective and celebrate your differences, whatever they may be. Think of them as yet another part of what makes you special. No matter what your physical issue, always believe in yourself. When you can stay strong and act confidently, your friends and classmates will respect you for it.

If you have classmates who are dealing with physical issues, I hope this book has helped you see them in a new light and better understand what they're going through. Starting to view people from a different perspective will not only help them—it might even earn you some new friends.

XOXO,
Stephanie

Pay It Forward

Remember, a healthful life is about balance. Now that you know how to walk that path, pay it forward to a friend or even to yourself! Remember the Get Healthy tips throughout this book, and then take these steps to get healthy and get going.

- When your body is in its best possible shape, you'll feel better about yourself. Eat a well-balanced diet filled with all the basic food groups (whole grains, fruits, vegetables, lean meats and fish, low-fat dairy). Also try to exercise for at least 60 minutes every day.

- Television and video games are fine—but only in moderation. Limit yourself to an hour or two a day. Then, turn off the tube or game console and find other activities that you enjoy.

- Pay attention when you go grocery shopping or eat in restaurants. Know what's in your food, including nutrients, fat, calories, and sugar.

- Get to know your body. Watch for warning signs, such as allergies, food sensitivities, or any other changes that might signal a problem.

- Form a partnership with your doctor. Go for regular checkups, ask questions, and follow your doctor's advice for staying healthy.

- If you're having trouble in school, work with your parents, teachers, and school guidance counselors to develop a learning style that works best for you.

- Learn how to relax. Practice yoga, meditate, listen to soft music, or just set aside some "me" time for yourself each day.

- Watch your words. If you are about to tease someone for any reason, stop for a second and think about how you'd feel if you were in his or her situation.

- Find a group of people you feel comfortable with. Look for people who share the same interests as you, and who accept you just the way you are.

- Always remember that you are beautiful, strong, and unique. Never let anything—or anyone—hold you back or prevent you from doing whatever it is you want to achieve.

Additional Resources

Select Bibliography

"Overview of Diabetes in Children and Adolescents." *National Diabetes Education Program.* May 2008. <http://ndep.nih.gov/diabetes/youth/youth_FS.htm#Type2>.

"Overweight and Obesity." *Centers for Disease Control and Prevention.* 18 Dec. 2008. <http://www.cdc.gov/nccdphp/dnpa/obesity/>.

"Recognizing an Asthma Attack." *American Academy of Pediatrics.* 1999. <http://www.medem.com/MedLB/article_detaillb.cfm?article_ID=ZZZE2O8XA7C&sub_cat=19>.

"Stuttering." *American Speech-Language-Hearing Association.* 2009. <http://www.asha.org/public/speech/disorders/stuttering.htm>.

Further Reading

Berger, William E., MD. *Teen's Guide to Living With Asthma.* New York: Facts on File, 2007.

Gallo, Donald R., ed. *Owning It: Stories About Teens with Disabilities.* Cambridge, MA: Candlewick, 2008.

Gordon, Sherry Mabry. *Peanut Butter, Milk, and Other Deadly Threats: What You Should Know About Food Allergies.* Berkeley Heights, NJ: Enslow Publishers, 2006.

Gunten, Sharon. *Learning Disabilities.* Farmington Hills, MI: Greenhaven Press, 2007.

Moran, Katherine J. *Diabetes: The Ultimate Teen Guide, It Happened to Me Series.* Lanham, MD: The Scarecrow Press, 2006.

Web Sites

To learn more about living with physical challenges, visit ABDO Publishing Company online at **www.abdopublishing.com.** Web sites about living with physical challenges are featured on our Book Links page. These links are routinely monitored and updated to provide the most current information available.

For More Information

For more information on this subject, contact or visit the following organizations.

American Academy of Allergy Asthma & Immunology

555 East Wells Street, Suite 1100
Milwaukee, WI 53202-3823
414-272-6071
www.aaaai.org
The AAAAI teaches adults and kids how to avoid and treat asthma and allergies.

American Diabetes Association

1701 North Beauregard Street, Alexandria, VA 22311
800-DIABETES (800-342-2383)
www.diabetes.org
The American Diabetes Association works to prevent the disease and to help those who already have diabetes.

Glossary

allergen
A substance such as pollen or pet fur that causes the immune system to react.

asthma
A disease in which the airway becomes narrow, making breathing difficult.

astigmatism
Blurred or distorted vision caused by a misshapen cornea in the eye.

cerebral palsy
A condition in which damage to the brain leads to difficulty with movement and speech.

cholesterol
A fatty substance that circulates in the bloodstream and can clog blood vessels.

choreographer
A person who creates dance moves.

diabetes
A disease in which the body does not produce enough insulin or does not use it effectively.

dyslexia
A learning disability that causes difficulty reading.

epinephrine
A chemical that is used to treat severe allergic reactions.

farsighted
Having trouble seeing objects that are close.

inhaler
A handheld device used to deliver medicine into the mouth of people with asthma.

insulin
A substance that helps the body turn sugars from food into energy.

lactose intolerance
Being unable to digest the natural sugar (lactose) in dairy products.

nearsighted
Having trouble seeing objects that are far away.

obese
Having too much body fat.

ophthalmologist
A doctor who treats the eyes.

ultraviolet
A type of light that comes from the sun.

wheezing
A whistling sound that can occur when people have trouble breathing, such as from asthma.

Index

About the Author

Stephanie Watson is a freelance writer based in Atlanta, Georgia. Over the years she has written for television, radio, the Internet, and print. Her books include *Daniel Radcliffe, Understanding Obesity: The Genetics of Obesity, What's in Your Food? Recipe for Disaster: Fast Food,* and *Living Green: Recycling.* She has been nominated for a National Online Journalism award and has won a PROMAX Silver award for television promotion.

Photo Credits

Fotolia, 12, 25, 58; Lee Morris/Shutterstock Images, 14; RJ Lerich/Shutterstock Images, 17; Kati Molin/Fotolia, 19; Anetta/Shutterstock Images, 27; Evgeny Dontsov/ Fotolia, 28; Monkey Business Images/Shutterstock Images, 35, 79; Armando Frazao/iStock Photo, 37; Terry Alexander/Shutterstock Images, 39; Lisa F. Young/ Fotolia, 45; Doug Olson/Fotolia, 47; Galina Barskaya/ Shutterstock Images, 55; Bondarenko/Shutterstock Images, 65; Barbara Laing/Getty Images, 69; Philip Date/ Shutterstock Images, 76; Philippe Minisini/Fotolia, 85; Fotolia, 86; Bernhard Richter/Fotolia, 89; Chris Schmidt/ iStock Photo, 95; Jaimie Duplass/Fotolia, 98